Starting Point for Understanding Mathematics
- Literature for Understanding Mathematics

Verity .E.

Starting Point for Understanding Mathematics
ISBN 9798718760972

Contents | Page

PREFACE

There are some basic (and simple) things about mathematics that are supposed to be known before someone can find mathematics easy to understand. Without first learning these certain 'simple things', mathematics would be strange and confusing. This book is intended to make mathematics understandable for all by presenting some basic simple things a student is supposed to learn first about mathematics so that things in usual mathematics would not be strange.

The book contains aspect of the subject that should make mathematics at High School level (Secondary School level) easy to understand: It contains aspect of mathematics that is important for understanding usual mathematics.

The book has been prepared as a reading material to help beginners in High School (Secondary School) to find mathematics understandable from the start, and also to help those finding mathematics difficult to understand at different levels to start finding the subject understandable.

Chapter 1

Introduction
Why Many Students Find Mathematics Difficult

Worldwide, mathematics is a subject that most students find difficult to understand at high school (secondary school) level. The problem usually starts when letters such as x, y, a, b and so on start appearing in mathematics books or on the school board. Use of symbols in the subject also makes math to look strange to many students. Many symbols are used in mathematics, for example: π, $\neq$, $\leq$, $\geq$, $<$, $>$, $=$, $\{\ \}$, $(\ )$, $!$ and many more. When a student does not understand the meaning of letters and symbols in a subject, as seen in mathematics, it is natural to find it difficult to understand what is seen in the subject or even much of the subject. This means that if the meaning of letters and symbols seen in mathematics are known to students including the reason why they are used in mathematics, then they should understand the subject or what they see in the subject.

Another problem is the way things are done when solving a problem in mathematics. Many students do not know how a teacher do things in mathematics to get an answer to a problem. They also do not know how students who are good in math do the things they do in math.

If you understand how things are done in mathematics, and the meaning of everything you see in mathematics, then you should be good in mathematics. This is because you would know how to do things by yourself in mathematics.

In chapters of this book, we will look into why letters (such as a, b, c, d, ... x, y, z)) are used in mathematics and how to use them. We will also see how things are done in mathematics. These will make mathematics not to be strange. This would enable a student to know how to do things in mathematics and be good in the subject.

Chapter 2

Why Alphabets are Used in Mathematics, and How they are Used

In early stages of school such as primary school level (or in early grade levels), in arithmetic everyone is familiar with things such as 1 + 3 = 4, and things such as 8 - 2 = 6. Things like these are familiar even in everyday life. Take note that 1 + 3 = 4 is short way to write a statement like: "one thing added to three things gives four things. Now consider the following statement: "I am thinking of a number. If I add it to five, I will get twelve. What is the number?"

This is supposed to be written as a simple arithmetic like as we wright 1 +3 = 4. But in the statement, it is said that "I am thinking of a number... So, what would we write as the number? It can be seen in the statement that the number is to be added to "five" and the result will be "twelve". In mathematics, when you do not know the exact number you are thinking of, we call such a number an *unknown number. In mathematics, when writing things, the general custom is to represent unknown numbers (or unknown things) with any alphabet of the English Language.* You have to choose any letter from a,b,c,d to z (the usual practice is to use small letters, though "capital" letters are also occasionally used) to represent an unknown thing. So, in the above example, if we are to write as in arithmetic, using usual short form, the words of the long statement would be replaced as follows: "five" is written as 5, the words 'if I add it' is written as '+', 'I will get' is written as '=', twelve is written as "12". The number I am thinking of can be represented with any letter of the English alphabets. Let us represent it with 'x' (meaning an unknown thing). So, in usual arithmetic form, the whole statement

3

will become: x + 5 = 12, what is 'x'. Take note that this is shorter than writing "I am thinking of a number, if I add it to five I will get twelve. What is the number?"

As said above, in mathematics, unknown things are usually represented with English alphabets. When for example you see something like this: b + 2c = y, it is saying that "a number (represented by "b"), when added to another number (represented by "c") multiplied by two, we will get an unknown number (represented by "y").

In mathematics, whenever you see an alphabet or alphabets inside written things, you should understand that the alphabets stand for unknown "numbers". If for example you see $\frac{68}{d}$ = 34, it is simply saying that "sixty-eight divided by a certain unknown number (represented by the letter 'd') gives thirty-four".

Also, if you have $\frac{u}{x}$ = y, it is saying that 'a certain number (represented by u) divided by another certain number (represented by x) will give another certain number (represented by y).

At this point, there is a fact you are to take note of: if they say "a certain number (represented by u) multiplied by another certain number (represented by v) gives, for example, ten, it could be written as u X v = 10. The fact to take note of is that when alphabets are involved in an equation that has a multiplication, the alphabets are simply written together without writing the sign of multiplication. For example, instead of writing u X v, we simply write uv (this is taken to be the same thing as u X v). The reason for using this method in mathematics is to avoid confusing the sign of multiplication 'x' to be an unknown when alphabets are involved. So, the rule in mathematics is that in use of alphabets to represent an unknown thing, if an alphabet is multiplying any other thing, the alphabet and the thing or things it is multiplying are simply written together without the sign of multiplication. So, when alphabets are involved, for example ux = d^3, note that they are all alphabets, (standing for certain unknown numbers) and none of them is a multiplication sign (that is when alphabets are used to represent unknown things). So, in ux = d^3, it means a certain unknown (represented by u) multiplied by another unknown (represented by x) gives another unknown (represented by d) raised to the power of three. We do not write them as

u X x = d^3. This can cause confusion. Someone might take the sign of multiplication as another unknown. We instead write it as ux = d^3 (here, there is only one 'x' and we know it is standing for an unknown number).

Some more examples: Instead of writing 6 x u = 24, in mathematics it is usually written as 6u = 24.

Instead of writing $\frac{8\,X\,f\,X\,n}{a\,X\,c}$, if the x stands for multiplication, we simply write $\frac{8fn}{ac}$. When things are written in mathematics, letter x is only used to represent an unknown number if a multiplication involves letters or symbols (it is not used as a multiplication sign in such situation). Take note that if the letter x in the above write-up is intended to represent an unknown thing, the above write-up would be written as $\frac{8xfxn}{axc}$.

But when addition or subtraction is involved, you have to write the signs (of addition or subtraction) appropriately. This is because they cannot be confused with any English alphabet (as the sign of multiplication may cause) when writing things that have alphabets. For example, you can write something like this $\frac{9a-n}{nb+c}$. This is saying nine multiplied by an unknown 'a', minus an unknown 'n', all divided by the unknown 'n' multiplied by an unknown 'b' and to which an unknown 'c' is being added. Once again, take note of how writing in words in mathematics can be longer than writing with just alphabets and symbols to represent things: **this is one reason mathematics is done with alphabets and symbols instead of with words!**

Take note of the above explanation so that you may not see alphabets as strange when you see them in mathematics writings. Though we know that when we have real numbers to add together such as 2 + 6, the addition is usually simple. In the case of 2 + 6 the answer is 8. This is usually written as 2 + 6 = 8. Subtracting, multiplying or dividing real numbers is usually straightforward too. But you may wonder how to handle letters in mathematics when they have to be added together, divided, subtracted or done some other ways as are usually done with numbers. This is not a problem. As you read this book further, you will learn how to handle letters in mathematics, and also how to handle symbols in mathematics. Luckily, handling of letters and symbols in mathematics are easy to learn; and learning these usually makes mathematics to become plain and understandable.

Chapter 3

THE USE OF SYMBOLS IN MATHEMATICS

Mathematics is a subject in which all writings are made as brief as possible. This is unlike most other subjects. In mathematics words are usually replaced with letters or with symbols. This is why letters and symbols are found in mathematics. In mathematics, you only first have to know what the symbols or letters stand for for you to understand what you see. This is a first aspect of the subject to take note of so as to understand all what you would be seeing in mathematics. As stated in the last chapter, there are advantages of using letters and symbols to represent words and statements in mathematics. Some advantages are: It makes mathematics writings brief, and also easier to handle compared to if things were to be done in complete words and statements in words.

Below here are some symbols you will frequently come across in ordinary level mathematics. There are many more symbols in mathematics. Always take note of what they mean whenever you come across them. As for the symbols hereunder, we shall state or explain what they are used to represent. Take note of their meaning as explained below so that whenever or wherever you come across them in mathematics you should understand what they stand for.

Some Symbols:

$\angle$ This is used to replace the word "angle". So instead of, for example, writing the word 'angle b', we simply write '$\angle$ b'. Note that it is shorter to use the symbol "$\angle$" than to write word "angle".

x: This is used to replace the word "multiply" or "multiplied by". So instead of, for example, writing 6 multiplied by 5, we simply write 6 x 5. The letter x is also used to represent an unknown in mathematics and in the sciences in general. When it is used to represent an unknown, the edges of the letter x are usually rounded as if it is a small letter form of it. In any situation, you will understand from the situation if it is representing a multiplication or representing something unknown.

∴ In mathematics this symbol is used to replace the word "therefore".

R (or, r): This is used to replace the word 'radius' when circles are being discussed. Note that *the radius of a circle simply means the distance from the center of the circle to any point on the surface of the circle.* The symbol 'R' is also used to represent 'rate' when discussing 'interest' (or 'simple interest'). From the above about the symbol 'R', you see that it is used to represent 'radius' when discussing circles and to represent 'rate' when 'interest' is being discussed. If circles are being discussed and you come across the symbol 'R' or 'r', (for example if they say r = 25cm) know that the 'r' here stands for the word 'radius'. But if the topic is about 'simple interest' or 'compound interest' and you come across the symbol 'R', then you should understand the symbol 'R' in this situation stands for 'rate'. *In mathematics, a particular symbol can be used to stand for a different thing in different topics or different situations. In any situation, what the symbol stands for is usually stated.*

+ This is a common symbol from elementary arithmetic. The symbol is used to replace the word 'plus' or 'added' or 'addition' or increase by'. For example, we do not write 8 plus 3. Instead, we write 8 + 3. It is shorter and quicker to use the symbol than to use the word "plus". The symbol known as "plus" might look ordinary, and one might wonder why it is included here. It is included here so that we should realize that it is actually a short form of the words "plus", "added", "add to" or "addition.

—   This symbol and "+" are commonly used symbols. It is used to replace the word "minus" or "remove" or "subtract". For example, instead of writing 'six minus two', we simply write 6 – 2. This is shorter and quicker.

÷   In mathematics this symbol is used to replace the words 'divide by'. For example, instead of writing 'twelve divided by two', we simply write it as 12 ÷ 2 (this is shorter). You may also see something written as $\frac{12}{2}$. The straight line between the 12 and the 2 is also used to replace the words 'divided by'. So $\frac{12}{2}$ simply means twelve divided by two. We also call it "ten over two". In this method of writing divisions in mathematics, the thing on top is known as the "dividend" (in our example $\frac{12}{2}$, the 12 is the dividend), while the thing below the line is known as the "divisor" (2 is the divisor in $\frac{12}{2}$). Take note that in mathematics, we prefer writing divisions in this form $\frac{10}{2}$ instead of in the form of 10 ÷ 2. So, you should be writing divisions in the form of $\frac{12}{2}$ (i.e., dividend over a divisor) instead of in the form of 12 ÷ 2. From these, if you come across things like the following $\frac{x}{d}$ or $^x/_d$ or x/d you should understand they are all cases of division, where one unknown thing is dividing another unknown thing. (It is in elementary school (primary school) mathematics where divisions are usually written in the form of 10 ÷ 2).

> This symbol is used to replace the words "is greater than". For example, instead of writing 'eight is greater than three', we simply write 8 > 3 (this is shorter as you can see).

< This symbol is used to replace the words "is less than". For example, instead of writing 'eight is less than ten', we simply write 8 < 10. (this is shorter). Take note of the difference between the symbol used to replace the word "angle" and the symbol for "less than". They are not the same. The symbol for 'angle' is $\angle$ and the one for 'less than' is <.

= This is used to replace the words "is equal to". So instead of saying in words (for example) that 'twelve is equal to ten added to two', we simply say $12 = 10 + 2$.

Remember we have said in this book that words are avoided as much as possible in mathematics. Things are written in symbols to make writing shorter and quicker. You just have to know what the symbols stand for and you will find mathematics to be plain and easy. The symbol '=,' was introduced (or started to be used) in the year 1557 by Robert Recorde to replace the words "is equal to". That was how the symbol '=' (two small equal lines to replace the words "is equal to") came into mathematics. Robert Recorde was a medical doctor and a teacher of mathematics. He was from the United Kingdom.

$\neq$ This is used to replace the words "is not equal to". For instance, instead of writing 'five added to two is not equal to nine', we simply write $5 + 2 \neq 9$. Take note that if you write $5 + 2 = 7$, it is correct, and if you write $5 + 2 \neq 9$ it is also correct because you are simply saying in the last case that five plus two is not equal to nine (which is literally true).

% In mathematics instead of writing the word "percent" (which means: "in every one hundred"), the symbol % is usually used to replace the words. So, if you see 60%, it means '60 in every one hundred' or '60 out of every one hundred'.

$\perp$ In mathematics, if a straight line stands upright on another line or on a surface, or if a straight line makes an angle of 90^0 (90 degrees) with another line or with a surface, we say the line is "perpendicular to" the other line or to the surface. The symbol $\perp$ is used to replace the words 'perpendicular to", because it is quicker to put the symbol down than to write the words.

$\triangle$ This symbol is used to replace the word "Triangle". In mathematics, instead of writing "triangle ABC" and "triangle DEF" for triangles such as shown below, we rather write "$\triangle$ABC" and "$\triangle$DEF" for short, using the symbol of triangle to replace the word "triangle".

If we have two triangles as shown below, or more than two triangles, we use the symbol of triangle with letter 's' inside it to stand for the word "triangles" as follows

For the triangles below, we would thus say $\triangle$sABC and DEF instead of the words 'triangle ABC' and 'triangle DEF'

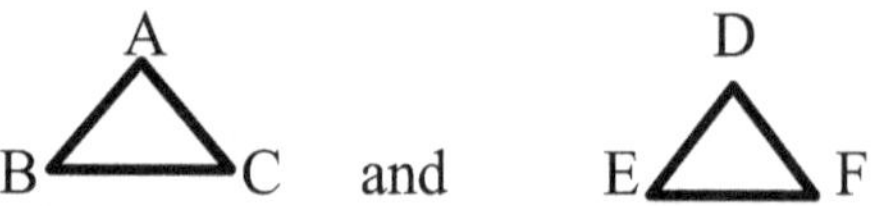

⌒   For every circle, a portion of the circumference of the circle such as from point A to point B as shown below is called an "arc".

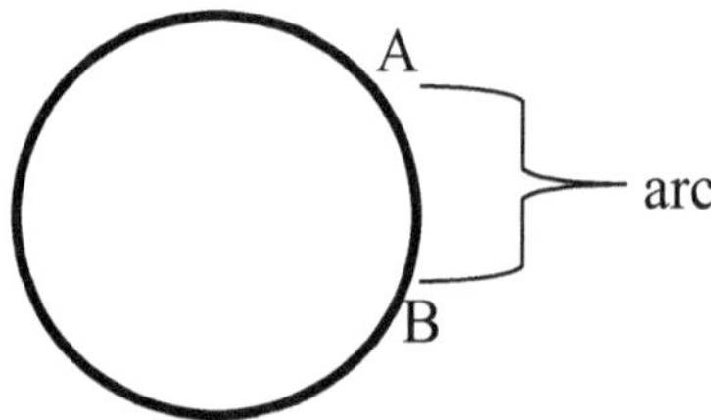

The symbol ⌒ is used to replace the word "arc". So instead of writing "arc AB", we simply write $\overset{\frown}{AB}$. When you see things like this $\overset{\frown}{CD}$ and $\overset{\frown}{AD}$ they mean "arc CD" and "arc AD".

( )   This symbol is known as brackets (the pair are the brackets; not only a single one of the two signs). They are used to show that everything contained by them are one group. If for example we have 6(n + 8 + v), it means six is multiplying a group of things as shown. *Take note that if a thing is multiplying a group of things, the sign of multiplication is not usually written.* The thing multiplying the group of things in the brackets is placed just near the brackets. Thus, we write 6(n + 8 + v), and not like this 6 x (n + 8 + v). This is to avoid confusing the sign of multiplication with an 'unknown thing' represented by alphabet 'x'. Take note of this information.

Also, if a group of things enclosed in brackets is multiplying another group of things enclosed in another brackets, you do not have to write out the sign of multiplication between the two groups. Simply state them as follows: (a − 8 + u)(3 - b), and not like this: (a − 8 + u) x (3 - b). But in case of a thing being added to a group of things, or being subtracted from a group of things, you have to write out the sign of addition or subtraction as the case might be. For example:

7 + (a − 8 + u). The seven is being added to the group of things. If we have 4 - (a − 8 + u) it means that the group of things is being subtracted from four. It was mentioned earlier that the sign of plus or the sign of minus cannot be confused as an unknown, as would happen with sign of multiplication which could be seen as unknown "x".

{ }   This symbol is known as the bracelets. They are also used in writing things into a group (i.e., in enclosing a group of things in mathematics). But usually, they are used in the following manner $3\{ 6 + c (8 − d)^2 \}$. You can see that there is a group of things in brackets as follows $(8 − d)^2$. And this group belongs to another group of things $\{6 + c (8 − d)^2\}$. The whole of this bigger group is being multiplied by 3 in the form of $3\{ 6 + c (8 − d)^2 \}$.

Usually, bracelets are used in writing things into a major group where there is a smaller group existing inside the major group. The smaller group is usually formed with brackets.

Take note that in writing things into groups, the first (inner) group is formed with brackets. The second group containing the first group and things outside the brackets is enclosed with bracelets.

[ ] This symbol is known as parenthesis. It is used in forming a main group that contains two smaller groups (formed by brackets and bracelets). So, parenthesis is used in the following manner $a^2[3\{b + c(8 - d)^2\}]$.

Take note that after using brackets, bracelets and parenthesis, if all the things are to be enclosed in a bigger fourth group we go on and re-use brackets as follows:

$9(a^2[3\{b + c(8 - d)^2\}])$. So, take note that in mathematics things *are not* written into a group using only brackets as follows: $9(a^2(3(b + c(8 - d)^2)))$. Instead, different symbols, the brackets, bracelets, and parenthesis are used alternately and repeated in that order if more groups are involved when writing things into groups in mathematics. At this point, you may check mathematics books to see the use of brackets, bracelets and parenthesis as explained here; Just a look into books to see what you have read here.

Mathematics has many symbols in use to represent some words, or to represent some natural facts. The symbols are used to avoid long writing in words. You should try to familiarize yourself with more symbols in mathematics and what they are used to represent. Always remember that symbols are used to make writings shorter.

Chapter 4

What Equations Mean in Mathematics

Look at the following statement:

'If you have a certain amount of dollars and add ten more dollars to it, you will have thirty dollars'

In the previous chapters of this book, it was stated that in mathematics writings are made as short or brief as can be possible to do. It makes things shorter to write down and easier to handle in the subject. As for the above statement about amount of dollars, in mathematics it is made shorter with use of symbols as:

$x + \$10 = \$30.$

Or $b + \$10 = \$30$

Any of the above is shorter to write, and tidy compared to the statement made in words. In the statement in words, the word "you will have" is replaced with the symbol "=" (the symbol of "equals to").

In mathematics, when a statement made in words is reduced to a short form with the use of symbols only (no words any longer) and especially with the presence of the sign of "equality", the writing is known as an equation. Simply, an equation is actually a statement written in symbols instead of in words. In mathematics, any statement presented in words is usually converted to a statement form in symbols. You will see later how this is done, and how to handle the symbol form of writing (that is how to handle an equation) to solve a problem.

So far in this book, you have seen why alphabets and symbols are used in mathematics, and what equations mean in mathematics (just statements made short with use of symbols).

Everything you see in mathematics books can be written in words, such that there would be no single symbol in mathematics; not even the signs of 'plus', multiplication, 'subtraction' etc. But if things are written in words (instead of the symbols you see), some mathematics books would be as big as ten Oxford Advanced Learners' dictionaries arranged on top of each other.

After things are written down in symbols with the sign of 'equals-to' connecting things on the left side to things on the right side, you can no longer say the things are a statement in words. No! It is no more a statement in words, but instead it is a statement in symbols. But the statement in symbols has the same meaning as the statement in words; it has just been made shorter with the use of symbols.

Important to know: After a statement is written in symbol form, it is called **an equation**. The word "equation" is used because things are being connected with the sign of 'equals-to' (i.e., things are being equated). So, *an equation is a statement made in symbols (instead of in words) and has the sign of 'equals-to' connecting things on one side of the sign of equals-to to things on the other side of the sign of equals-to.* Equations are used in mathematics (instead of words) to make writings shorter.

Mathematics is not some form of tricks or magic. Everything in mathematics has real meaning in words. Symbols are used to make writing of things shorter, and things are also handled in symbols.

From all what has been said, it is clear that one can decide to write something down in words or in symbols (an equation). For example, consider the following situation: 'I have forty-nine goats, but I owe somebody three goats. So, in all I have forty-six goats. Instead of writing a statement in words like that, it could be written in symbols and made shorter as follows: 'my number of goats is $49 - 3 = 46$. This is shorter. The statement in symbols means exactly the same thing as the statement in words. For example, in the above writing in symbols, we mean that you have 49 and you owe 3. Therefore, in reality you only have 46. So, you can see that equation and statements in words really say the same thing; only that an equation speaks in short or brief symbols while a statement speaks in words, which are longer to write down. But always bear in mind that in an equation, the symbols are things used to replace words of a statement, and the entire equation is a statement in words that has been reduced to only symbols. This replacement is done to make things shorter and quicker to write. Let us consider another example of how to convert a statement into an equation.

Look at the following statement: 'James is twice as old as John, and the sum of their ages is sixty'. This is a statement in words. If you decide to write it in the form of symbols (that is an equation), you have to represent the essential words with symbols before putting the symbols together to form an equation. You may do it as follows: let the age of John be 'x'. So 'x' will replace the words 'age of John'. An alphabet is used because the age of John is not yet known as a number ('x' is used here, but any alphabet could also be used). Now if James is twice as old as John, since you have already represented the age of John with 'x', so twice the age of John will be the same as 'twice x'. (You have to replace the word 'twice' with the symbol '2', so 'twice x' would be written as '2x'). So, we say John is 'x' years old and James is '2x' years old. In the statement you are trying to change into and equation form, it is mentioned that the sum of their ages is sixty. So, John's age plus James age equals sixty. In symbols, it is $x + 2x = 60$. Here, 'x' is John's age and '2x' is James age. You have replaced everything with symbols and have changed the statement into the form of an equation (to make the statement shorter in writing, using symbols instead of words).

That is the nature of writings in mathematics. And solutions for problems are also carried out step by step working with symbols. Always look at every equation you see in mathematics as a statement (about certain things) that is written as brief as possible using symbols.

Chapter 5
How to Form Equations

Knowing how to form equation from a given statement is important. In physics, chemistry and other subjects where use of mathematics is usually involved, questions are frequently presented in the form of a statement in words. Before you can work many of such problems, you have to change a question that is given in words into the form of equation, using symbols to replace words. In other words, you have to replace the essential words with symbols and then convert the whole statement or question into a statement in symbols (i.e., into an equation). Remember we said that an equation is a statement where the essential words have been converted into symbols, and thus presented in the form of a statement made with symbols instead of words.

When you change a statement in words into a statement in symbols with a sign of "equality" (=), you have formed an equation. If you know how to do this, you should eventually find physics, chemistry and all the sciences easy.

Read the following carefully

If you are given any question in words or a statement in words, read it carefully; take note of all the things mentioned. Try to understand the question or statement to the point that you can explain what is being asked (or stated) to another person. If you can explain what is being asked, or stated, then you really understand what is before you. If you find it difficult to understand a question or a statement, read it again carefully and check if there is an English word or expression you are not sure of the meaning. If there is a word you are not sure of the meaning, check for the meaning in an English language dictionary. After that, read the question or statement again and be sure you understand it enough to be able to explain it to another person.

When reading the question or statement, bear in mind that any number written in words would have to be replaced with the symbol form of it. This is to say: one, two, three and so on will have to be replaced with the symbol forms: 1, 2, 3 and so on. Also, anything the quantity of which is not surely known or stated is to be replaced with any 'letter' (or an alphabet). You can decide to use any from among a, b, c, d…to z. But note that once you use an alphabet to represent something, if another unknown is mentioned you have to use another alphabet to represent the different unknown (unless there is a stated relationship between it and a previously mentioned unknown). Let us look at an example: 'I am thinking of two numbers, if they are added together we get twenty-five'. If we are to convert this statement in words into an equation form, looking at the statement you will notice that two numbers are first mentioned and that when added together gives twenty-five. The two numbers are not mentioned in value, so they are unknown, (and there is no mentioned relationship between them; like maybe one is twice or three times the other); and so, we have to represent them with alphabets. Let one of them be 'a' and the other be 'b'. It is mentioned that the sum of the two numbers is twenty-five. Since twenty-five is a known number, we write it in its symbol form '25'. Also replace 'added together' with the symbol '+', and the words 'we get' with the symbol '='. We have done necessary replacements with symbols. So, we can proceed to write the original statement made with words as a shorter statement in symbols as follows: $a + b = 25$.

You can see that forming an equation from a given statement or from a given question is a simple procedure. Everything in mathematics could be simple if you understand the basic facts about them.

In replacement of unknown things with alphabets, if in one way or another a particular unknown thing is mentioned twice in a statement or question, you have to use the same alphabet to represent that particular unknown thing. For example, if it is said that 'I have a certain number, if I add it to twenty-four the result will be the same as when I multiply it by four': if we are to convert the statement in words into a shorter form using symbols (i.e., into an equation), we can represent the 'certain number' with any letter. Let us call it 'm'. So, adding it to twenty-four will be written as 'm + 24. Multiplying it with four will be 'm x 4'. Since the statement says adding the number to twenty-four gives the same answer as when it is multiplied by four, the symbol form of the whole statement will be m + 24 = m x 4. This is the same as m + 24 = 4m. From the written equation, you can see how the same alphabet could be used more than once to represent an unknown thing if the unknown thing is mentioned more than once in a statement or question. In the statement above it is said that the unknown number when added to twenty-four gives the same result as when it is multiplied by four. You can see that the unknown thing is to be added to twenty-four, and the same unknown thing is to be multiplied by four. So, the particular unknown thing occurred twice in the statement; we represent it with a letter and use it in the different ways it occurred in the statement.

From the examples given so far, you should be able to form an equation from a given statement of words or from a question given in words.

Let us consider another example: 'This year the sum of the ages of Sam and Tom is thirty-six. Nine years ago, Tom was twice as old as Sam'. Take note of an important information at this point: to convert a statement in words to a statement in symbols, pay attention to everything mentioned in the statement or question, and include everything when writing the new brief statement (the equation you are forming) so that it will be a real brief form of the entire statement. Usually, everything mentioned are part of the statement, so they remain relevant. Let us now look into the example above. It is mentioned that 'nine years ago Tom was twice as old as Sam'. Facts mentioned in a statement are useful when writing in symbols (that is when forming an equation). So, let us say the age of Sam nine years ago was 'x', then the age of Tom nine years ago will be '2x' because he was twice as old as Sam nine years ago. But if Sam was 'x' years old nine years ago, this year he will be 'x + 9' years old. As for Tom, if he was '2x' years old nine years ago, this year he will be '2x + 9' years old. Further, it is mentioned that this year the sum of their ages is thirty-six. This is to say, this year, 'Sam's age + Tom's age = thirty-six'. Or in complete symbols,

$$(x + 9) + (2x + 9) = 36.$$

Sam's age ———— Tom's age

Assuming you looked at the statement at the beginning and took it that if the sum of their ages this year is 36, then nine years ago the sum was $36 - 9 - 9 = 18$. (the first 9 is from Sam's age, and the second 9 is from Tom's age). Then, since it is mentioned that Tom was twice as old as Sam in that nine years ago, if Sam was 'x' years old nine years ago, Tom would be '2x' years old in nine years ago. Since the sum of their ages nine years ago is 18, as we worked it out above, then $x + 2x = 18$.

This is also correct like as we got in the previous working where we got

$(x + 9) + (2x + 9) = 36.$

They might look different in appearance but, in reality, they are the same. You will understand how they are the same in meaning as you learn more things in this book.

What matters in forming a statement in symbols (forming an equation) from a statement or a question given in words is to approach it from any way of reasoning and take everything mentioned in the statement into your plan to form a statement in symbols.

So far you have learned what an equation is, and how to form equation from a statement that is given in words. Forming equation from a statement is very important because in the sciences and other subjects where mathematics or calculations are involved, many problems are usually given or come in words. You have to read the statements or questions carefully first, and have to convert everything into a form in symbols (form an equation first) before proceeding to work on the problem.

Read everything in this chapter again before going on to the next chapters.

Exercise 1

Look at the following statements carefully and write an equation about each of them.

(1) If you add four to a certain number you will get eleven.

(2) The difference between two numbers is equal to the sum of the first one and Ten.

(3) James is three times older than Bill. The sum of their ages is thirty-six.

(4) The difference between certain two numbers is equal to what you will get if you divide the first one by Four.

Chapter 6

Some Basic Important Things to Know About Equations

It was mentioned earlier that in an equation, usually there is a sign of 'equals-to' and there are things on the left side of it, and other things on its right side. The sign of 'equals-to' or sign of equality (this sign "=") is what connects the things on the left side to the things on the right side of an equation. See below.

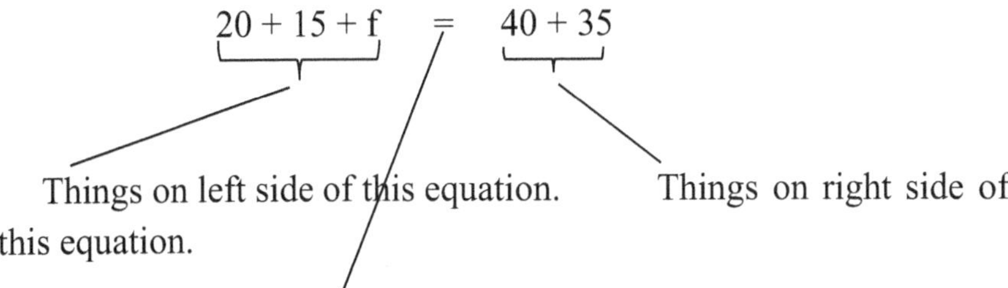

This sign of 'equals-to' connects things on the left side of the equation to things on the right side of the equation. This shows that everything on the left side together as one equals everything on the right side together as one. This is an important fact to take note of concerning every equation. The fact means a lot in mathematics.

There are some other important facts you must know concerning equations. These will be listed below. They are simple facts, and they are not many. They are like secrets of mathematics; with knowledge of them, you should be able to easily handle calculation problems in mathematics, physics, chemistry, economics and in any other subject that involves calculations. The simple facts when understood enable every student to be capable of handling equations and calculations with ease. **The facts are as follows:**

(1) Facts about the symbol of '+' and the symbol of '-' in an equation.

In any equation, for example a + b − c + 3 = 8, the symbol of '+' or of '-' is a part of the thing next to it. For example in the equation a + b − c + 3 = 8, the symbol of '+' written before the 'b' is a part of the 'b'. This is to say +b is a single thing in the equation. The '+' and the 'b' are not separate. You do not consider them as separate. Also, the '− c' is one thing, so also is the '+ 3'. It is a fact you should know here about the symbol of 'plus' and the symbol of '-' in an equation. This means that you can decide to remove '+b' or '- c' etc., or do anything to them in the equation; but you do not handle only the '+' separately from the 'b', neither do you handle only the '-' separately from the '3'. Things that are together are handled together! Meanwhile, there is one thing that must be mentioned here. If you look at the equation above again, you will notice that on the right side of the equation there is only one thing, (the number 8) and it has no sign of 'plus' or 'minus' on it. It is written as just 8. Also, on the left side of the equation the first figure is 'a'. It has no sign of plus or minus on it. An important fact you should know here is that in any equation, if a thing is alone on one side of the equation (like the 8 in the equation above) and it has no sign of plus or minus before it, it actually has a sign of plus that is usually not written. Also, if a thing is the first in an equation (like the 'a' in a + b − c + 3 = 8), if there is no sign before it, it actually has a sign of plus on it but it is usually not written. These are rules in mathematics, just to make writing further shorter. If the first thing in an equation has no sign of plus or minus written before it, then understand that it has a sign of plus. But if it has a sign of minus, it must be written before it. The same applies for anything standing alone on one side of an equation. So, the above equation is actually $+a + b - c + 3 = +8$. But as a rule or way of writing in mathematics, it is written as $a + b - c + 3 = 8$. For an equation that has a minus on its first thing or on a thing standing alone on one side of the equation, the sign of minus must be written (it is a rule in mathematics). You will see such equations with signs of minus written, for example, as follows $- y + c - d = 9$. Let us look at a few more examples.

$$3 + 9 = 19 - 7.$$

From what you have learned above about the symbols of plus and minus in an equation, you should look at this equation as actually being: $+3 + 9 = +19 - 7$.

If you have $- 9 - 3 = y + z - u$, it is actually $- 9 - 3 = + y + z - u$.

If you have $u + v = y$. This is actually $+ u + v = + y$.

(2). Next fact to take note of:

Look at the following different equations:

(i) $23 - b + \dfrac{y}{z} = u + 9a$

(ii) $- x \mid b = 18$

(iii) $v = \dfrac{a}{t} + 1$

(iv) $x^2 - b = -4 + c$

(v) $\sqrt{a} = 2c$

Looking at the equations above, you can see the signs of plus, minus, multiplication (2c on the right side of equation (v) is actually 2 multiplying c and +9a in the first equation is actually +9 multiplying a), and the sign of root (this sign $\sqrt{}$ in equation (v)), sign of power (x is raised to power of 2 in equation (iv)) and division (in equation (i) we wrote y ÷ z like this $\frac{y}{z}$. This is a division. The same with $\frac{a}{t}$ in the third equation).

What you are to known here is that in every equation you will come across in basic mathematics, the signs of plus, minus, multiplication, division, roots and powers are the common signs you will see now and then with numbers or alphabets etc. This is important to keep in mind because you will later learn how to handle these signs in an equation when working a problem.

(3). Next fact to know about equations.

We mentioned earlier that in an equation, there is a sign of 'equals-to' (the sign of equality) which connects the left side to the right side of the equation. This sign means that everything together on the left side of an equation equals everything together on the right side of the equation. Take note we mean everything together! If the things on both sides of the equation were to be stones, it means that to maintain the sign of equality, if you remove any stones from the left side, you must remove the same number of stones from the right side. If you add to one side, you must add the same number to the other side for the two sides to remain equal. Whatever you do to one side you must do the same to the other side to keep the two sides remain equal. If not done this way, the sign of equality will become wrong to be in the equation. The point is that whatever you do to one side of an equation, you must do the same to the other side of the equation so as to keep the two sides remain equal. This fact makes a simple sense. But it is a very important fact in mathematics, because when handling any equation in mathematics or in other subjects for any reason, it makes somebody to be careful and always do the same thing to both sides of an equation so as to keep both sides of the equation remaining equal (as indicated by the sign "="). Let us look at some examples.

Let us consider the following equation $x + 3 - b = 9 + c$

If you square the left side of the equation, you must also square the right side of the equation so as to keep the two sides remain equal. In such a case we would have $(x + 3 - b)^2 = (9 + c)^2$.

Assuming you add something to the right side, for example let us add 8 to the right side. You must add the same thing to the left side to keep the two sides remain equal (as indicated by the sign: =). We will have $x + 3 - b + 8 = 9 + c + 8$. If you subtract anything from one side of the equation, you must subtract the same thing from the other side of the equation to keep the two sides remain equal. Let us for example subtract 'u' from the left side, and we do the same to the right side. We will have $x + 3 - b - u = 9 + c - u$.

If for any reason you decide to divide one side by anything, you must also divide the other side by the same thing so as to keep the two sides remain equal.

So long as you have the sign of 'equals-to' still there, you must make sure you keep the two sides remain equal by doing whatever you do to one side of the equation to the other side of the equation.

Talking about division of one side of the above equation we are considering, if for example you decided to divide the left side by 'n' for any reason, you must also divide the right side by 'n' so as to keep the two sides remain equal. We will have

$$\frac{x + 3 - b}{n} = \frac{9 + c}{n}$$

If for any reason you decided to find a 'root' of one side, whatever your reason for doing it to the 'one side', you must do the same to the other side of the equation for the purpose of keeping the two sides remain equal. For example if you decide to find the third root of the right side as follows, $\sqrt[3]{9+c}$, you must do the same to the left side. So you end up having the equation becoming like this: $\sqrt[3]{x+3-b} = \sqrt[3]{9+c}$.

The equation remains correct because you have been careful to keep the two sides remain equal.

That is how to do things with equations in mathematics because of the sign of equality; and you can understand it is a proper way to treat equations so that the two sides will remain equal as indicated by the sign of 'equals to'. We have above here used the words 'if for any reason you decided to do something to one side of an equation'. There are times you may decide to do something to one side of an equation for some reason or for some reasons. As we move into more chapters of this book, you will come to see how such situations can arise. Whenever such a situation arises that for some reason you must do something to one side of an equation in mathematics or any other subject, just make sure you do the same thing to the other side of the equation to keep the two sides of the equation stay equal.

Things are "marked" as incorrect in mathematics when you fail to keep the two sides of an equation remain equal when handling an equation or when solving a problem in mathematics.

Chapter 7

How to Solve Problems in Mathematics
(How equations are handled to solve a problem)

In mathematics (or in questions that have calculation in other subjects) when problems are given, one is usually asked to find something, or solve for something or find the value of something etc. In solving for something or finding something, the thing you are solving for or 'finding' has to be made to remain alone on the left side of an equation (or alone on one side of an equation) and every other thing is made to be on the other side of the equation. For example if you are given $\chi + \dfrac{f}{2} = v - 1$ and you are asked to find 'f', it means you should make only 'f' to remain on one side of the equation. You are to make it to remain alone on the left side of the equation. That is the usual practice. And it is reasonable like that because you are going to say 'f' is 'equal-to' so and so and so. (Or in symbol form $f = \ldots$). So, after working on the equation or solving it, at the end only the 'f' should be on the left side and every other thing is to be on the right side of the equation. The summary is that, in working a problem, at the end you have to make the thing you are looking for (the answer) to be on the left side of the equation, and every other thing that is still in the equation has to be made to be on the other side of the equation.

But how is someone supposed to work a problem in mathematics?

This is going to be explained thoroughly next.

First of all, take note that to leave only what you are solving for on the left side of an equation means that you have to remove every other thing from that side. But you do not just keep the other things anyway you like it on the other side of the equation. The sign of 'equals-to' shows that in an equation, everything on one side (together) equals everything (together) on the other side. So, there are right ways to remove or move things or re-arrange things in an equation so as to make sure the two sides of the equation remain equal. The methods are not many; they are simple, and interesting too – just the matter of knowing the few ways. Once you know the simple ways of doing this, mathematics becomes an easy subject. They will be explained in simple understandable language hereunder.

How to correctly remove things from one side of an Equation so as to leave what you are looking for (or solving for) alone on that side of the equation.

The method of *correctly removing* things from one side of an equation in mathematics is based on the idea that whatever you do to one side of an equation, you must do the same to the other side of the equation, so as to keep the two sides remain equal. Mark the word 'correctly'; not just 'removing'. Read the sentence above again. For example, if you have $6 + 9 = 15$, you cannot just remove 9 from the left side without doing the same to the right side of the equation and expect the two sides to remain equal. I mean you cannot remove the 9 from the left side only and say $6 = 15$. You can see that this is not right; 6 things are not equal to 15 things when talking about <u>similar</u> things (for example money, 6 pounds is not equal to 15 pounds, or for similar fruits, 6 oranges = 15 oranges. These are not right). So, to keep the two sides equal in $6 + 9 = 15$, if you are removing 9 from the left side (for any reason), you also must at the same time remove 9 from the right side. This will keep the two sides remain equal. You do it like this: $6 + 9 - 9 = 15 - 9$. Remember that to remove is to 'minus', that is why we write '$- 9$'. If you look at the two sides of the equation, you will see that the result will become $6 = 6$. You know $6 = 6$ is correct. This is how to handle an equation to keep the two sides remain equal - for the equation to remain correct. The summary is that whatever you do to one side of an equation, you must do the same to the other side of the equation so as to keep the two sides remain equal.

If you keep this in mind always, you will know how to act right at every step when removing things from one side of an equation to get what you are looking for (while still keeping the equation correct as far as the sign of 'equals-to' is concerned).

Now, to look for something (or solve for something) in an equation is like an interesting action: you just start to remove every other thing one by one from the left side of an equation so as to leave what you are looking for alone on the left side of the equation. You only just have to be careful to keep the two sides remain equal; by making sure whatever you do to anything on the left side of the equation so as to remove it from there, you must do the same thing to the other side of the equation so as to keep the two sides of the equation remain equal. You go on with the game until you have only what you are looking for on the left side of the equation (or alone on one side of the equation).

Look at the following problem: $x + 8 = 21$, find 'x'.

From all what you have read above, you should now know that to find 'x' in this equation means that one is supposed to make 'x' to be alone on the left side of the equation while other things have to be on the other side of the equation. You can see that on the left side we have x + 8. So we have to remove the +8. This is simple; put − 8 on that same side so that it will remove the +8 (you know that +8 − 8 will give zero for the two of them. And this means you have removed the +8). Just make sure that as you put minus8 on the left side, you must put minus8 on the right side of the equation to keep the two sides remain equal as explained earlier above.

So, x + 8 = 21, to find 'x', we do as follow:

x + 8 − 8 = 21 − 8

∴ x + 0 = 13

(You know that 1 + 0 gives 1, also 2 + 0 gives 2; so understand that x + 0 will be 'x', just like z + 0 will be 'z')

So, X = 13 Ans. Take note that "Ans" is short form of the word "Answer".

Before we proceed from here, take note of the following: To add something is to "plus" something and to remove something is to "minus" something. So to remove something that has a "+" is simply done by putting in a similar thing but that has a minus.

Common Symbols in Equations

The common symbols you see in an equation in connection with numbers and alphabets are $+$, $-$, x, $\div$, $\sqrt{}$ (the sign of root), / or — (line signs of division). There could also be a symbol of 'raised to a power', for example such as 8^2 (8 raised to power 2, also known as 8 squared) and X^3 (x raised to power 3) etc. In some equations, some other symbols with their own meaning could be found. Now let us look at an equation and take note of the symbols in it

$x + 7 - \dfrac{u}{v} = 9 + a$. You can see that on the left side of the equation, there are the symbols of $+$, $-$ and division (the ''u'' is being divided by ''v''). On the right side of the equation there is ''+'' symbol. TAKE NOTE that the equation is saying x <u>plus 7,</u> <u>minus u,</u>(which is <u>divided by v</u>) equals-to 9 <u>plus 'a'.</u> An important thing to know here is that there is 'x', there is '+7', there is '-u', there is '/v'(which is the same thing as 'divided by v'), and there is '9' and '+a'. You can see that each symbol is attached to the alphabet or number that you write after you write the symbol. So there is '+7' (the plus belong to the 7 written next to it), there is divided-by-v (the division symbol belongs to the 'v') and there is '+a'.

That is the nature of equations. So if you want to remove the '7' in the equation above, you should know that the '7' is not alone; it is '+7'. Also, the 'u' is not just 'u'; it is '−u'. The 'v' is actually '/v'. The 'a' is '+a'. What of the 'x' on the left side of the equation, and what of the'9' on the right side of the equation? Are they just 'x' and '9' like that? The answer is 'NO'. We said earlier that in equations, if the thing beginning the equation has no symbol written before it, it means it has the symbol '+'. So in our equation above, the 'x' on the left side of the equation is actually '+x', and the '9' on the right side of the equation is actually '+9'.

So, to remove '+7' from the left side of the equation, you have to simply put '−7' on that same side so that it will take away the '+7'. It is like saying 7 − 7. You know what that means. But remember to also put '−7' on the right side of the equation so as to keep the two sides of the equation remain equal (you are maintaining the equality of the two sides). (If the '7'in the equation were to be a '−7', you would have had to put in a +7 so as to remove the −7). In the same way, to remove the '+x' from the left side, you have to put '−x' on the left side. That will take away the '+x' from the left side (remember to also put '−x' on the right side of the equation too, to keep the two sides remain equal). You now know how to go about removing a number or a letter from any side of an equation if the number or letter has a '+' symbol or a '-' symbol.

A question: How do you remove a number or an alphabet from any side of an equation if the number or alphabet has a 'multiplication' symbol or a 'division' symbol or a 'root' symbol ($\sqrt{}$) or a symbol of 'raised-to–a-power'?

Just as we use a 'minus-something' to remove a thing that is a 'plus-something' from any side of an equation when handling an equation, any number or alphabet with the other symbols such as a multiplication, '÷', '$\sqrt{}$' etc. have a way for easily removing them from any side of an equation. As a thing with the symbol of minus ('−') is used to remove a similar thing having the symbol of '+', so is a thing with the symbol of 'multiplication' is used to remove a similar thing that has the symbol of 'division'. This information must be kept at heart, and never thrown away.

Remember the case of removing a number or anything that has a '+'. For example, if you have y + 8 = 17, and you are asked to find 'y', you will say, remove the 8 from the left side to leave the 'y' alone, and also remove 8 from the right side so as to keep the two sides remain equal. So you will say:

y + 8 = 17

y +8 −8 = 17 − 8

(+8 − 8 gives '0', and 17 − 8 gives 9)

So, y + 0 = 9

∴ y = 9.

How to remove a thing that has a division symbol

In a case of having to remove a thing that has a division sign from one side of an equation, let us look at the following: $\frac{y}{8}$ = 2, find y. Take note that we have to remove 8 from the left side to leave the 'y' alone on that side,

The 8 is dividing the 'y'. So the 8 has a division sign with it. To remove a thing that has a division symbol, we have said above that we have to put in a similar thing that has a multiplication symbol. In this case now, we would go on like this: multiply the left side by 8 so as to remove the 8 that is dividing the 'y'. Also multiply the right side by 8 so as to keep the two sides remain equal.

So, $\dfrac{y}{8} \times 8 = 2 \times 8$

$\dfrac{y}{\cancel{8}} \times \cancel{8} = 2 \times 8$

y = 16.

The "eights" are cancelled, to show they are removing each other.

That is how to target anything that has a division symbol with it, and remove it with a similar thing that has a multiplication symbol. If it were to be a thing that has multiplication symbol that you want to remove from one side of an equation, you have to use a similar thing that has a division symbol. It is just like the case of 'plus' and 'minus' symbols that are used against each other when removing something from an equation. The symbols of 'division' and 'multiplication' are used against each other when removing a thing that has one or the other of them from an equation.

A case of removing something that has a multiplication symbol or that is multiplying another thing.

9y = 27, find 'y'.

To find 'y', you are supposed to do something to remove the '9' from the left side of the equation so as to have only the 'y' on the left side of the equation.

You can see that the 9 is multiplying the 'y'. It is actually 9 multiply y = 27. We said earlier that in mathematics, if a number is multiplying a letter or any other thing which is not a number, the sign of multiplication is not usually written. The things are written like this: 9y, 7b, 8π, and so on. We all know they are multiplications though multiplication sign is not written. So the things above here are actually 9 x y, 7 x b, 8 x π and so on.

For 9y = 27, to find y, you now know that the 9 is multiplying the 'y'. So to remove the '9', we divide the left side by '9', and do the same thing to the right side of the equation to keep the two sides remain equal.

We would have, $\dfrac{9y}{9} = \dfrac{27}{9}$.

$$\dfrac{9y}{9} = \dfrac{27}{9}$$

$$\therefore y = \dfrac{27}{9} = 3.$$

Another Example: $\dfrac{x}{u+v} = y$. Find 'x'.

We can see that 'x' is being divided by 'u + v' together. So we should remove the 'u + v' together by multiplying the left side by 'u + v'. We also have to multiply the right side by 'u + v' so as to keep the two sides remain equal.

So, for $\dfrac{x}{u+v} = y$. To find 'x'.

$$\dfrac{x}{u+v} \text{ multiplied } (u+v) = y(u+v)$$

$$\dfrac{x}{u+v} \text{ multiplied } (u+v) = y(u+v)$$

$$\therefore x = y(u+v)\ldots..\text{Ans.}$$

Removal of roots ($\sqrt{\ }$, $\sqrt[3]{\ }$, $\sqrt[4]{\ }$ ...) and things with 'powers (4^2, y^3, x^4...or n^x and so on)

You already know that in removing things from any side of an equation, a thing with symbol of 'minus' is used to remove a similar thing that has a symbol of 'plus', and a thing with symbol of 'plus' is used to remove a similar thing that has a symbol of 'minus'. Also, 'division' action is used to remove a 'multiplication' thing from an equation. And a 'multiplication' action is used to remove a 'division' thing. It is clear here that 'plus' and 'minus' are used against each other and 'multiplication' and 'division' are used against each other when removing things from an equation. In the same way, 'ROOTS' and 'POWERS' are used against each other when removing things from an equation (in mathematics a power is many-times multiple of something; a root is many times reduction of something). The reason for all these is the fact that we use the exact opposite of something to remove the 'something'. For example, 'minus' is the opposite of 'plus'. So, if for example, we have $6 + 2 = 8$, to remove $+2$ from the left side of the equation we have to put in -2 on that side of the equation. The left side of the equation will become $6 + 2 - 2$. The $+2$ will become removed. You have to also put -2 on the right side of the equation so as to keep the left side and the right side remain equal. So, we will have $6 + 2 - 2 = 8 - 2$. If this is worked out, we find that the two sides of the equation will remain equal, even as the 2 on the left side is removed. It is all about removing something from one side of an equation, while still keeping the two sides of the equation remain equal and correct. So, talking about using the opposite of a thing to remove a thing, 'minus' is the opposite of 'plus', 'multiplication' and 'division' are opposites of each other, and 'power' and 'root' are opposites of each other.

Look carefully below here to see how a case of 'roots' and 'powers' is done:

If for example you have $y^3 = 27$, and you are asked to find 'y',

You have to remove the power of '3' from the 'y^3' so as to get the 'y' you are looking for.

Remember we just said that to remove a thing with 'power', we use a similar 'root' against it. In the example we have here, the 'power' the 'y^3' has is power of '3'. So we have to use root '3' to remove the power of '3'. Root '3' is called 'cube root' or in symbol it is $\sqrt[3]{}$. To use it to remove the power of '3' we put-it-in like this: $\sqrt[3]{y^3}$

.

But remember that whatever you do to one side of an equation you must also do it to the other side of the equation so as to keep the two sides remain equal. So in this case we must put $\sqrt[3]{}$ over everything on the right side of the equation to keep the two sides remain equal.

So we have $\sqrt[3]{y^3} = \sqrt[3]{27}$.

The cube root can now remove the third power on the y^3 as below:

$$\sqrt[3]{y^3} = \sqrt[3]{27}$$

$$y = \sqrt[3]{27}$$

But $\sqrt[3]{27} = 3$

So y = 3.

What you have learned above here are the methods used in handling equations to solve problems in mathematics. (They are the methods used in removing things from any side of an equation when solving for something in an equation, so that what you are solving for will be what is left alone on one side of the equation).

Chapter 8

Some Important Facts About Equations

Some important facts to know concerning equations that have things with division, multiplication, addition, subtraction, roots and powers

(1) If you have something like 3 – 2, it is the same thing as -2 + 3. Remember we said earlier in this book that when you see something written as 3, it actually means +3. So, 3 – 2 is actually +3 – 2 and you can also write it as -2 + 3. It will give the same answer if you work it out. The reason is 3 – 2 means 'add three and remove two. This will give 1. And – 2 + 3 means remove two and add three. This also means getting 1. So, 3 – 2 and – 2 + 3 gives or mean the same thing. Similarly, a – b is the same thing as –b + a. A reason why you have to know this fact is that if, for example, you have something like x – 2, if you want to remove the - 2 you would have to simply put +2 on that side of the equation to have x – 2 + 2. The -2 + 2 is the same as +2 – 2 or 2 – 2. This will result in zero, leaving only the x alone on the side of the equation that has them. This fact will help you to know what to do when handling or trying to remove things that have the signs of '+' or −.

(2) **Look at the following equation**: $\frac{x}{2} + 6 - b = 16$, find 'x'. If in any given problem what you are to solve for is one of the things

involved in division on one side of the equation, and there are other things on that same side of the equation which are not involved in the division, then there is something you have to know so that you do not make mistakes. What you are to know here is that before you touch the things that are involved in the division, you should first remove every other thing that is not involved in the division from that side of the equation. For example, in the problem $\frac{x}{2} + 6 - b = 16$, before you touch the $\frac{x}{2}$ you have to first remove every other thing from that side of the equation. This means you have to first remove the $+6$ and the $- b$ from that side of the equation. So, let us first put $- 6$ on the left side of the equation to remove $+ 6$ from that side of the equation (we also have to put $- 6$ on the right side of the equation so as to keep the two sides remain equal).

So,

$$\frac{x}{2} + 6 - 6 - b = 16 - 6$$

This gives $\frac{x}{2} + 0 - b = 16 - 6$

$$\frac{x}{2} - b = 10$$

Next, put $+b$ on the left side of the equation to remove $- b$ from that side. Also remember to put $+b$ on the right side so as to keep the two sides of the equation remain equal.

$$\frac{x}{2} - b + b = 10 + b$$

$$\frac{x}{2} + 0 = 10 + b$$

$$\frac{x}{2} = 10 + b.$$

It is when you have things involved in a division standing alone on one side of an equation, as you now see above, that you can go on to touch the things involved in the division when handling an equation. At this point we can proceed as follows.

Continuing from $\frac{x}{2} = 10 + b$.

(Multiply the left side with 2 so as to remove the 2 that is dividing the 'x'. Remember to also multiply the entire right side by 2 so as to keep the two sides remain equal)

$$2(\tfrac{x}{2}) = 2(10 + b)$$

$$2(\tfrac{x}{2}) = 2(10 + b)$$

$$\therefore x = 2(10 + b).$$

We have just seen how to do things when solving for something that is a part of division in an equation. The same approach is used if what we are solving for is a part of a multiplication in an equation. Let us use one equation as an example of a situation where what we are solving for is involved in a multiplication inside an equation.

Assuming we have $3x - b + a = 30$, (to find 'x', as the problem), you can see that 'x' is a part of '3x' in the equation. '3x' is a case of multiplication. '3' is being multiplied by 'x'. Before we touch the '3x' to get 'x', we must first remove everything that is not multiplying (or that is not dividing) the 'x' from that side of the equation. In other words we have to first remove the −b and +a from the left side of the equation before handling 3x to get 'x'.

So, $3x - b + a = 30$

Put +b on the left side of the equation to remove –b from the left side (also remember to put +b on the right side of the equation to keep the two sides remain equal).

$3x - b + b + a = 30 + b$

$3x + 0 + a = 30 + b$

$3x + a = 30 + b$

Next put –a on the left side of the equation to remove +a from that side (also remember to put –a on the right side of the equation to keep the two sides remain equal).

$3x + a - a = 30 + b - a$

$3x + 0 = 30 + b - a$

$3x = 30 + b - a$

We can now divide the left side by 3 so as to cancel out (remove) the 3 on that side to leave only the 'x' on that side since we are looking for 'x'. We also have to divide the right side by 3 so as to keep the two sides remain equal.

So, $\dfrac{3x}{3} = \dfrac{30 + b - a}{3}$

Cancel as appropriate $\dfrac{\cancel{3}x}{\cancel{3}} = \dfrac{30 + b - a}{3}$

We do the 'Cancel' because we know the two things have to go since they have been arranged to go.

$$\therefore \; x = \frac{30 + b - a}{3} \quad \text{Ans.}$$

Once again, if you have something like $2x + \dfrac{3}{v} - ab = 6 + c.$ (find x)

What you are asked to find is not part of $+\dfrac{3}{v}$ or $-ab$. It is rather attached to 2 in the form of '2x'. This means you must first remove the $+\dfrac{3}{v}$ and the $-ab$ from the left side of the equation as they are not part of what you are looking for (what you are looking for is inside '2x'). You can remove the $+\dfrac{3}{v}$ from the left side of the equation by putting $-\dfrac{3}{v}$ on that side of the equation (also put $-\dfrac{3}{v}$ on the right side of the equation so as to keep the two sides remain equal).

$$2x + \frac{3}{v} - ab = 6 + c$$

$$2x + \frac{3}{v} - \frac{3}{v} - ab = 6 + c - \frac{3}{v}$$

$$2x + 0 - ab = 6 + c - \frac{3}{v}$$

$$2x - ab = 6 + c - \frac{3}{v}$$

Put +ab on the left side of the equation to remove the $-ab$ on that side. Also put +ab on the right side of the equation so as to keep the two sides of the equation remain equal.

$$2x - ab + ab = 6 + c - \frac{3}{v} + ab$$

$$2x + 0 = 6 + c - \frac{3}{v} + ab$$

$$2x = 6 + c - \frac{3}{v} + ab.$$

You can now divide the left side by 2 so as to remove the 2 that is multiplying the letter x. Also divide the right side of the equation by 2 so as to keep the two sides remain equal.

$$\frac{2x}{2} = \frac{6 + c - \frac{3}{v} + ab}{2}$$

$$\frac{\cancel{2}x}{\cancel{2}} = \frac{6 + c - \frac{3}{v} + ab}{2}$$

$$\therefore \quad X = \frac{6 + c - \frac{3}{v} + ab}{2} \quad \text{Ans.}$$

Two important points here above, which you have to keep at heart, is that before you multiply a side of an equation so as to remove something that is involved in a division, or before you divide one side of an equation to remove something that is involved in a multiplication, as the case might require, you have to first remove other things that are not involved in the division or the multiplication from that side of the equation appropriately.

Examples on Removal of Things from a Side of an Equation When Solving a Problem

You have learned how to remove a thing that has a plus sign from one side of an equation when solving for something or handling an equation. You have also learned how to remove a thing that has a minus sign, and also how to remove a thing that is multiplying another thing or things and how to remove a thing that is dividing another thing or things. You have also learned how to remove the signs of roots and the signs of powers from things in an equation. Let us now work some examples on these things you have learned so far, to further make you see more on them.

Examples on removal of things bearing the sign of 'plus': Follow the examples below here carefully to increase your skills.

Example (1): $x + v = y - 1$ find 'x'.

(To find 'x', you have to remove the '+v' from the left side of the equation to leave only the 'x' you are looking for).

To remove the +v, simply put −v on the left side of the equation. This will make +v to be out of that side of the equation because we will have x + v − v becoming x + 0 (remember that +v − v will give zero and that is how we have x + 0). Also remember to put −v on the right side of the equation so as to keep the right and the left sides of the equation remain equal.

So, $x + v - v = y - 1 - v$

$X + 0 = y - 1 - v$

$\therefore x = y - 1 - v.$ Ans.

Example (2). Solve for 'n' in the following equation: $b + n + 2 = 3$.

To solve for 'n', every other thing on the left side of the equation is to be removed from that side of the equation so as to leave the 'n' alone on that side of the equation. This means the '+b' and the '+2' are to be removed from the left side of the equation. To remove the '+2', you have to put '−2' on the left side of the equation, because +2 − 2 will give zero and so the +2 will be gone from the left side of the equation. Meanwhile, also put '−2' on the right side of the equation so as to keep the left and the right sides remain equal.

So, b + n + 2 − 2 = 3 − 2

b + n + 0 = 3 − 2

b + n = 3 − 2

to remove 'b' from the left side,

b − b + n = 3 − 2 − b

0 + n = 3 − 2 − b

n = 3 − 2 − b

n = 1 − b   Ans

Example (3): a + b +c(u − v) = x, solve for 'a'.

You can see that there are brackets in this equation (on the left side of the equation) on the side of the thing we are to solve for. But the thing we are to solve for, the 'a', is not inside the brackets. Also, it is not multiplying the brackets and it is not dividing the brackets. At this point, take note of the following: if what you are to solve for is not inside brackets and it is not multiplying the brackets, and if it is not dividing the things in the brackets, then you can regard the brackets and everything inside it (with anything that is multiplying it, if there is any, and anything dividing it, if there is any) as one single thing. And so, you can remove everything inside the brackets with the brackets together from that side of the equation as one single group of things.

So, in the equation a + b + c(u − v) = x, you are to handle +c(u − v) as one thing. You have to put −c(u − v) into that side of the equation so that +c(u – v) and –c(u –v) will give zero (and so we would have removed the +c(u – v). Meanwhile, remember to also put –c(u –v) on the right side of the equation so as to keep the two sides remain equal.

But if what you are solving for is inside brackets in a given equation, then you have to must open the brackets before you can solve for the thing you are to solve for. We shall see an example of such a situation later.

To solve for 'a' in a + b + c(u – v) = x

Put –c(u – v) on the left side of the equation to remove the + c(u – v). Also at the same time put - c(u – v) on the right side of the equation so as to keep the two sides remain equal.

a + b + c(u – v) – c(u – v) = x –c(u – v)

a + b + 0 = x – c(u –v)

a + b = x – c(u – v)

put –b on the left side of the equation so as to remove the +b on the left side (also put –b at the same time on the right side of the equation so as to keep the two sides remain equal).

a + b – b = x – c(u – v) – b

a + 0 = x – c(u – v) – b

∴ a = x – c(u – v) – b.   *Ans.*

Example (4):

n + 2(d + c) = 8, Find 'd'.

Put –n on both sides of the equation (this will keep the two sides remain equal, while the one on the left side will remove the +n on that side).

n – n + 2(d + c) = 8 – n

0 + 2(d + c) = 8 – n

2(d + c) = 8 – n

Divide the left side of the equation by 2: this will remove the 2 that is multiplying the brackets. Also divide the right side of the equation by 2 so as to keep the two sides of the equation remain equal.

$$\frac{2(d+c)}{2} = \frac{8-n}{2}$$

Cancel out the 2 on the left side of the equation

$$\frac{\cancel{2}(d+c)}{\cancel{2}} = \frac{8-n}{2}$$

$$d + c = \frac{8-n}{2}$$

Remove +c from the left side of the equation

$$d + c - c = \frac{8-n}{2} - c$$

$$d + 0 = \frac{8-n}{2} - c$$

$$d = \frac{8-n}{2} - c \qquad \text{Ans.}$$

Example (5):

$$u + \frac{v}{a} = f \quad . \text{ Solve for 'u'.}$$

You can remove the $+\frac{v}{a}$ from the left side of the equation as one single thing.

Remember that is how to treat things which are dividing themselves if what you are looking for is not inside them.

So, put $-\frac{v}{a}$ on the left side of the equation so as to remove $+\frac{v}{a}$ from that side of the equation. Also, at the same time, put $-\frac{v}{a}$ on the right side of the equation so as to keep the two sides remain equal.

So, for $u + \frac{v}{a} = f$

$$u + \frac{v}{a} - \frac{v}{a} = f - \frac{v}{a}$$

$$u + 0 = f - \frac{v}{a}$$

$$u = f - \frac{v}{a}. \qquad \textit{Ans.}$$

Example (6):

$$n + ab = c, \text{ find 'n'.}$$

Handle +ab as a single thing since what you are solving for is not part of +ab. So, to remove +ab, put –ab on the left side of the equation so as to remove +ab from that side of the equation. Also put ab on the right side of the equation so as to keep the two sides of the equation remain equal.

$$n + ab = c$$

$$n + ab - ab = c - ab$$

$$n + 0 = c - ab$$

$$n = c - ab. \quad \textit{Ans.}$$

Example (7):

Solve for 'b' in the following. $u + b + cd + \frac{n}{x} + 2(e - h) = f - v$

In this problem, you are to solve for 'b'. So you have to remove every other thing from the left side of the equation one after the other until only the 'b' will remain alone on one side of the equation. Remember, that is the usual way of solving for something.

So, $u + b + cd + \frac{n}{x} + 2(e - h) = f - v$

Put -2(e – h) on the left side of the equation so as to remove +2(e – h) from that side of the equation. Also at the same time put -2(e – h) on the right side of the equation so as to keep the two sides remain equal.

$$u + b + cd + \frac{n}{x} + 2(e - h) - 2(e - h) = f - v - 2(e - h)$$

These will result in zero

So, $u + b + cd + \dfrac{n}{x} + 0 = f - v - 2(e - h)$

$$u + b + cd + \frac{n}{x} = f - v - 2(e - h)$$

Put $-\dfrac{n}{x}$ on the left side of the equation to remove $+\dfrac{n}{x}$ from that side of the equation. Also put the same thing on the right side of the equation so as to keep the two sides stay equal.

$$u + b + cd + \frac{n}{x} - \frac{n}{x} = f - v - 2(e - h) - \frac{n}{x}$$

$$u + b + cd + 0 = f - v - 2(e - h) - \frac{n}{x}$$

$$u + b + cd = f - v - 2(e - h) - \frac{n}{x}$$

Remember you are solving for 'b'. So keep removing things from the left side of the equation where the 'b' is, until only the 'b' is left there. Put $- cd$ on the left side of the equation to remove $+cd$ from that side. Also put $- cd$ on the right side of the equation so as to keep the two sides remain equal.

$$u + b + cd - cd = f - v - 2(e - h) - \frac{n}{x} - cd$$

This will result in zero

$$u + b + 0 = f - v - 2(e - h) - \frac{n}{x} - cd$$

$$u + b = f - v - 2(e - h) - \frac{n}{x} - cd$$

Put '− u' on the left side of the equation so as to remove '+u' from that side. Also put '− u' on the right side so as to keep the two sides remain equal.

$$u - u + b \;=\; f - v - 2(e - h) - \dfrac{n}{x} - cd - u$$

$$\text{So, } 0 + b \;=\; f - v - 2(e - h) - \dfrac{n}{x} - cd - u$$

$$\therefore b \;=\; f - v - 2(e - h) - \dfrac{n}{x} - cd - u \qquad \textit{Ans.}$$

Examples on removal of things bearing the sign of Minus

Solve for 'L' in the following: $L - u = d + v$.

To remove the '− u', you have to put '+u' on the left side of the equation. As you do so, also put '+u' on the right side of the equation to keep the two sides remain equal.

Example 1:

$$L - u = d + v$$

$$L - u + u = d + v + u$$

This will give zero

$$L + 0 = d + v + u$$

$$L = d + v + u \qquad \textit{Ans.}$$

Example 2:

c – a – d = 8b, find 'c'.

To solve for 'c', you have to remove '–a' and '–d' from the left side of the equation to leave only 'c' on that side of the equation. To remove '–d' from the left side of the equation, put '+d' on the left side of the equation. Also put '+d' on the right side of the equation to keep the two sides remain equal.

So, c – a – d + d = 8b + d

This will give zero.

c – a + 0 = 8b + d

c – a = 8b + d

Put '+a' on the left side of the equation to remove '–a' from the left side. Also put the same thing on the right side to keep the two sides remain equal.

c – a + a = 8b + d + a

This will give zero.

So, c = 8b + d + a   *Ans.*

Example (3):

u – ab – n = 1. Find 'u'.

You have to make the 'u' be alone on one side of the equation. So, remove '–ab' and '–n' from the left side of the equation. Put +ab on the left side of the equation so as to remove –ab from that side of the equation. Also put +ab on the right side of the equation so as to keep the two sides remain equal.

$$u - ab + ab - n = 1 + ab$$

This will give zero.

so, $u - n = 1 + ab$

Put +n' on the left side of the equation to remove −n from the left side. Also put +n on the right side of the equation so as to keep the two sides remain equal.

$$u - n + n = 1 + ab + n$$

This will give zero.

So, $u = 1 + ab + n$ Ans.

So far, you should have noticed how we 'put-in' something into an equation to remove something. After putting something on one side of an equation, you also see how you must put the same type of thing or things into the other side of the equation so as to keep the two sides remain equal. We have seen how putting something into one side of an equation results in zero or removes the thing we want to remove or eliminate. From the next example on, we will assume you already know how the zero happens, or how the removal happens. So we might no longer mention "these results in zero" or "put the same thing on the other side of the equation so as to keep the two sides remain equal". Just take note that we would be doing things to remove things from one side of an equation so as to leave only what we are solving for. Very important; take note that whatever we do to one side of an equation, we do the same to the other side of the equation so as to keep the two sides remain equal as we go on solving for something. Let us now look at another example.

Example (4):

$$x - \frac{a}{y} - d = n, \text{ find 'x'.}$$

You have to make 'x' to remain alone on one side of the equation. So, you have to eliminate other things from the left side of the equation.

Remove '– d' from the left side of the equation:

$$x - \frac{a}{y} - d + d = n + d$$

$$x - \frac{a}{y} + 0 = n + d$$

$$x - \frac{a}{y} = n + d$$

Now, remove $-\frac{a}{y}$ from the left side of the equation.

$$x - \frac{a}{y} + \frac{a}{y} = n + d + \frac{a}{y}$$

$$x + 0 = n + d + \frac{a}{y}$$

$$\therefore x = n + d + \frac{a}{y} \quad \text{Ans.}$$

Examples of solving for a thing that is multiplying another thing, or that is multiplying other things

Example (1):

U + ab = x. find 'a'.

From what you have seen done in this book concerning how to handle equations, you should know how to solve for 'a' in the example here. Watch how we proceed from here to find 'a'.

U + ab = x

U – U + ab = x – U

0 + ab = x – U

ab = x – U

Divide the left side of the equation by 'b' so as to eliminate 'b' from 'ab' to leave only 'a'. Also divide the right side of the equation by 'b', so as to keep the two sides remain equal.

$$\frac{ab}{b} = \frac{x - U}{b}$$

$$\frac{a\cancel{b}}{\cancel{b}} = \frac{x - U}{b}$$

$$\therefore a = \frac{x - U}{b} \qquad \text{Ans.}$$

Example (2):

$$2ax = \frac{z}{c}. \quad \text{Solve for x.}$$

To remove '2' and 'a' from the left side of the equation to get 'x', divide the left side by '2a' so as to cancel (eliminate) the '2a' that is multiplying 'x' on the left side. Also divide the right side of the equation by '2a' so as to keep the two sides remain equal.

$$\frac{2ax}{2a} = \frac{\frac{z}{c}}{2a}$$

Next, cancel out the '2a' on the left side of the equation. This actually means 'divide '2ax' by '2a' on the left side of the equation.

$$\frac{\cancel{2ax}}{\cancel{2a}} = \frac{\frac{z}{c}}{2a}$$

$$\therefore x = \frac{\frac{z}{c}}{2a} \text{Ans.}$$

Examples of solving for a thing when it is inside things that are dividing themselves

Example (1):

$$\frac{a}{b} = x. \quad \text{Find 'a'.}$$

You can see that we have to eliminate 'b' from the left side of the equation so as to get just 'a'. The 'b' is dividing the 'a'. So, if you multiply the left side by 'b', it will eliminate the 'b' from the left side of the equation. We also have to multiply the right side of the equation by 'b' so as to keep the two sides remain equal.

$$\frac{a}{b} = x$$

$$\frac{ab}{b} = bx$$

$$\frac{a\cancel{b}}{\cancel{b}} = bx$$

$$a = bx \qquad \text{Ans.}$$

Example (2):

$$\frac{x}{uy} = n. \text{ Find x.}$$

Following what you know about handling equations,

$$\frac{uyx}{uy} = uyn$$

$$\frac{\cancel{uy}x}{\cancel{uy}} = uyn$$

$$x = uyn \quad \text{Ans.}$$

So far, we have explained a number of things about equations in mathematics including how to handle equations. We have shown how to handle 'unknown' things (represented by alphabets etc.) that have the signs of 'plus', 'minus', or that are involved in multiplication or division in an equation when we are solving for something.

Some simple but important facts to know in mathematics

The following are some other important things to note. Knowledge of them would be useful when solving some problems in mathematics.

Look at the following: $\dfrac{\frac{24}{3}}{2}$. This is 24 divided by 3, and all is further divided by 2. You know that 24 divided by 3 gives 8, and 8 divided by 2 will give 4. So, to work $\dfrac{\frac{24}{3}}{2}$ you can first work $\dfrac{24}{3}$ and further divide the answer by 2. You will have $\dfrac{\frac{24}{3}}{2} = \dfrac{8}{2} = 4$.

Look at another case $\dfrac{\frac{40}{2}}{5}$. To work it, you may proceed as follows:

$$\dfrac{\frac{40}{2}}{5} = \dfrac{20}{5} = 4.$$

But at this point, notice something about the two examples we have just considered above: looking at the first one, $\dfrac{\frac{24}{3}}{2}$, if you use the 2 which is the lower denominator to multiply the 3 which is the first denominator that is dividing the 24, you will have $\dfrac{24}{3 \times 2} = \dfrac{24}{6} = 4$.

This is the same answer you got when you divided 24 by 3, and further divided the result by 2.

Let us try the same approach with the second example: if you use the second denominator which is 5 to multiply the first denominator which is 2, you will have $\frac{40}{2 \; x \; 5} = \frac{40}{10} = 4$. This is also the same as the answer you got when you first divided 40 by 2 and further divided the answer by 5. *What is to be noticed here in mathematics is that when handling equations (or in calculations involving equations) if you have something like $\frac{\frac{90}{5}}{8}$, you can simply re-write it as $\frac{90}{5 \; x \; 8}$. You will still have the right answer when you work it out, just as you noticed in the two examples above.* This implies that if you have something like $\frac{\frac{x}{a}}{y}$ you should simplify (make it simple) as $\frac{x}{a \; X \; y}$ or simply as $\frac{x}{ay}$.

So, $\frac{\frac{x}{a}}{y} = \frac{x}{ay}$.

If you have something like $\frac{\frac{15}{6}}{3}$, handle it as $\frac{15}{6 \; X \; 3}$.

It is a useful fact you should take note of. On page 46 we worked $2ax = \frac{z}{c}$ to find x. We arrived at: $x = \frac{\frac{z}{c}}{2a}$. This is not supposed to be left this way. We are supposed to further write the answer as $\frac{z}{c \; X \; 2a} = \frac{z}{2ac}$.

More on how to Remove a Root (such as this $\sqrt[n]{}$) from things in mathematics

A root could be square root ($\sqrt{}$), cube root ($\sqrt[3]{}$) or any other root. Let us say it could be n^{th} root (n^{th} root means any root whatsoever). So, how to remove n^{th} root means how to remove any root whatsoever. Let us first consider square root.

We have shown that the opposite of a 'root' is a 'power'. For example the opposite of a **square root**, written as this $\sqrt{x}$, is a **square** which is usually written as x^2, where 'x' means any number whatever, e.g. 3^2, 4^2 and so on. From this reality, to remove just **a root** from a thing or a group of things, we use **a power** equivalent of the root to do the removal. We do it as follows:

Example: Given this $\sqrt{36}$, remove the square root from the $\sqrt{36}$.

Solution:

To remove the **sign of square root** from $\sqrt{36}$,

Put the **sign of square** on it as follows $(\sqrt{36})^2$

Putting a square removes a square root as follows;

$(\sqrt{36})^2$. This gives the 36.

Considering more examples, if you are given $\sqrt{a} = x$ and for some reason you are supposed to remove the square root from $\sqrt{a}$ to get 'a'. From what you have learned, you are to go about it as follows:

$\sqrt{a} = x$

Square the left side of the equation so as to remove the square root from $\sqrt{a}$ to get 'a', also square the right side of the equation so as to keep the two sides of the equation stay equal (the two sides will stay equal because you squared both sides, and not only one side of the equation);

We would have $(\sqrt{a})^2 = x^2$

The square on the left side of the equation and the square-root on the same left side of the equation would remove themselves (we have already seen above that a square removes a square root):

so, $(\sqrt{a})^2 = x^2$.

$a = x^2$ Ans.

Another example:

given that $\sqrt{u + v - t} = 8 + \text{x}$. Remove the square root from the items on the left side of the equation.

To do this, square the left side of the equation and also square the right side of the equation to keep the two sides stay equal, while the 'squaring' will remove the square-root on the left side of the equation:

$$(\sqrt{u + v - t})^2 = (8 + x)^2$$

$$(\sqrt{u + v - t})^2 = (8 + x)^2$$

$\therefore u + v - t = (8 + x)^2$.

Another example:

if you have $\sqrt{u + v - t} + \frac{1}{4} - v = 9 + x$, and for some reason you are to remove the sign of square-root from the things under it, proceed as follows:

$$\sqrt{u + v - t} + \frac{1}{4} - v = 9 + x$$

First remove everything that is not under the sign of square-root from the left side of the equation. This is because you have to have only the things under a root on one side of an equation before you start targeting the root. It is usually easy that way. Proceed to first remove the other things one after the other from the left side of the equation. You may start with any such items. Starting with removal of 'v':

$$\sqrt{u + v - t} + \frac{1}{4} - v = 9 + x$$

$$\sqrt{u + v - t} + \frac{1}{4} - v + v = 9 + x + v$$

$$\sqrt{u + v - t} + \frac{1}{4} + 0 = 9 + x + v$$

$$\sqrt{u + v - t} + \frac{1}{4} = 9 + x + v.$$

Next remove $+\frac{1}{4}$ from the left side of the equation to remain only the things under the sign of root on that side.

$$\sqrt{u + v - t} + \frac{1}{4} - \frac{1}{4} = 9 + x + v - \frac{1}{4}$$

$$\sqrt{u + v - t} + 0 = 9 + x + v - \frac{1}{4}$$

$$\sqrt{u + v - t} = 9 + x + v - \frac{1}{4}$$

Now we have only things under the sign of a root on one side of the equation. We can now proceed to remove the sign of root.

$$\sqrt{u + v - t} = 9 + x + v - \frac{1}{4}$$

$$(\sqrt{u + v - t})^2 = (9 + x + v - \frac{1}{4})^2$$

Everything on both sides have been squared so as to keep the two sides stay equal while at the same time the square on the left side will remove the square-root from the items under it.

$$\text{Next, } (\sqrt{u + v - t})^2 = (9 + x + v - \frac{1}{4})^2$$

$$u + v - t = (9 + x + v - \frac{1}{4})^2$$

You sure now know how to remove the sign of square root when handling an equation. But what of the sign of 'cube root' ($\sqrt[3]{}$), '4th root' ($\sqrt[4]{}$) or any other root whatsoever which we may call n^{th} root? What method is used to remove these other roots?

The fact is that whatever the root, the method is exactly the same.

So, if for example you have $\sqrt[3]{27} = x$, to remove the cube-root from $\sqrt[3]{27}$, just as we did in the case of square-root, you have to 'cube' both sides of the equation (this means you have to raise both sides of the equation to the 'power of three') as follows:

$$(\sqrt[3]{27})^3 = x^3$$

On the left side of the equation above, the 'power of three' brought-in will remove the sign of 'cube-root' as follows:

$(\sqrt[3]{27})^3 = x^3$

$\therefore 27 = x^3.$

If you have $\sqrt[3]{a}$ = n, and you are to remove the 'cube-root' from $\sqrt[3]{a}$. You go about it in the same way as follows:

$(\sqrt[3]{a})^3 = n^3$

$(\sqrt[3]{a})^3 = n^3$

So, a = n^3.

If you have $\sqrt[3]{y} = 9$, and you are to remove the sign of cube root from $\sqrt[3]{y}$ to get only 'y' on the left side of the equation, you go about it as follows:

$\sqrt[3]{y} = 9$

$(\sqrt[3]{y})^3 = 9^3$

y = 9^3.

Let us consider an example of a 4th root. If for instance you have $\sqrt[4]{x}$ = 10, and you are to remove the 4th-root from $\sqrt[4]{x}$ to get only 'x' on the left side of the equation, you are to go about it the same way:

$\sqrt[4]{x} = 10$

$(\sqrt[4]{x})^4 = 10^4$

$$\left(\sqrt[4]{x}\right)^4 = 10^4$$

$$x = 10^4.$$

In a case of any other root, the method is the same. Let us consider a case of nth root.

If we have $\sqrt[n]{y} = 50$, and we are asked to (or for some reason have to) remove the nth root from the $\sqrt[n]{y}$ to have only 'y' on the left side of the equation, we go about it as follows:

$$\sqrt[n]{y} = 50$$

$$(\sqrt[n]{y})^n = 50^n$$

$$\left(\sqrt[n]{y}\right)^{\cancel{n}} = 50^n$$

$$y = 50^n.$$

In mathematics, when letters are used in equations, we handle them just the way we would handle numbers. This way, we keep our mind on how we would do it if it were to be numbers instead of letters.

Another example: remove the sign of 9th-root from things under it on the left side of the following equation

$$\sqrt[9]{a + b + c} - \frac{2}{6} = f + 1.$$

From what you already know so far, you go about it as follows:

$$\sqrt[9]{a + b + c} - \frac{2}{6} = f + 1$$

First remove the $-\dfrac{2}{6}$ from the side that has the 9th-root so as to have only the 9th-root with the things under it alone on one side of the equation.

$$\sqrt[9]{a+b+c} - \dfrac{2}{6} + \dfrac{2}{6} = f + 1 + \dfrac{2}{6}$$

$$\sqrt[9]{a+b+c} + 0 = f + 1 + \dfrac{2}{6}$$

$$\sqrt[9]{a+b+c} = f + 1 + \dfrac{2}{6}$$

Now that the things with the 9th-root are alone on one side of the equation, proceed to remove the 9th-root by putting a 9th power on both sides of the equation

$$\left(\sqrt[9]{a+b+c}\right)^{9} = \left(f + 1 + \dfrac{2}{6}\right)^{9}$$

Next use the 9th power to cancel out the 9th-root on the left side of the equation. $\left(\sqrt[9]{a+b+c}\right)^{9} = \left(f + 1 + \dfrac{2}{6}\right)^{9}$

So, $a + b + c = \left(f + 1 + \dfrac{2}{6}\right)^{9}$.

In conclusion, you have learned how to remove the sign of a root (whatever the root) from a thing or things in an equation in mathematics. You should be able to remove a root, if the need be, when solving for something in mathematics or when handling an equation.

Exercise 2

(1) $5v + v = g$ Find v

(2) $8h = n - c$ Find h

(3) $\frac{a}{b} + k = d$ Find k

(4) $\frac{g}{u+v} = d$ Find g

(5) $tu = \frac{u+v}{v}$ Find t

(6) $2at + n = w$ Find t

(7) $\sqrt{x} = af$ Find x

(8) $\sqrt{u + c} = d$ Find u

(9) $\sqrt{2a} = u$ Find a

(10) $\sqrt{dn - x} = 25$ Find n

(11) $\sqrt[3]{c} = at$ Find c

(12) $\sqrt[3]{a - d} = x$ Find a

(13) $\sqrt[4]{u + 3} = ab$ Find u

(14) $\sqrt[n]{a} = du$ Find a

(15) $a^2 = 9$ Find a

(16) $u^2 + 2as = v^2$ Find u

(17) $a^n = c$ Find a

Chapter 9

TYPES OF PROBLEMS IN MATHEMATICS

This chapter is about how problems are usually presented in mathematics.

Problems in mathematics are usually presented either in the form of equations or in the form of a statement in words.

Problems that are in the form of equation

When a problem is given in the form of equation, one may be asked to "solve for something" or "find something" etc. It comes down to being expected to make one thing in an equation to stand alone on one side of the equation, while any other thing or things present in the equation are to be made to be on the other side of the equation. You are to make sure the left side of the equation stays equal to the right side of the equation as you do all what you do to get to your final point. As already said many times in this book, this means for each thing you do to one side of the equation as you proceed, you must do the same to the other side of the equation. This is except when you do a simplification on any side of the equation (making the side simpler; for example, if you have something like 2+4 on one side of, or inside an equation, you may choose to "simply" write 6 in their place so as to tidy up the place). We have pointed out that to solve for something or find something in an equation, you have to eliminate every other thing from that side of the equation one after the other. We have treated the ways of eliminating things from any side of an

74

equation; things that have the signs of '+', '–', division, roots and anything that has the sign of 'power' on it. You should study these again in previous chapters of this book. When you master how to carry out each of them, then you have come into mathematics. You should from that point onward understand books on mathematics; topic on mathematics and things you are taught in mathematics class. How to eliminate things bearing the signs mentioned here above are simple (as you see it done in previous chapters of this book). You may again study the previous chapters of this book where they are treated.

How to solve problems that are in the form of a statement in words

In the sciences and in mathematics, many problems are usually given, or come, in the form of a statement in words. You are told certain things or given some information and you are to calculate something or find something etc. When problems are given in words, they at times look confusing. But you are to look at them with the mindset of trying to understand what is being said. Do not try to get the answer outright; rather try to first understand **what is being said** and **what is being asked**. The next move is to try to convert the statement into an equation (a statement in symbols). This was treated earlier in this book. You may go back to the chapter to refresh your knowledge on how to form an equation from a statement made in words. In the form of an equation, a problem is usually easier to handle. An equation makes plenty grammar in words to become compact and no-longer confusing. Once you create an equation from a statement made in words, you would at once see how to proceed to get an answer to any question raised in the statement.

Let us consider some examples of problems that are given in words.

Example: The sum of the ages of Amos and Sam is 86 years. Amos is four times older than Sam. How old is Amos?

If you attempt to figure out the answer to a problem given in words, it could be confusing or difficult to do. Getting answer is usually easier or more convenient through handling equation. So make sure you master how to form equation from a statement given in words. As already said, how to form equation from a statement in words was treated earlier in this book.

Considering the problem we have here, it is stated that the sum of the ages of Amos and Sam is 86 years. The exact age of each of them is not given. So their individual ages are unknown. The first step here is to represent their ages with alphabets. (It was stated earlier in this book that in mathematics an alphabet or a letter is used to represent something that is not yet known).

A very important trick to know here is: to use an alphabet to represent one 'unknown' and then look for a connection between the things mentioned in the given statement and use that connection to form any other 'unknown' item. This is an important way of forming equation from a given statement. For example in the problem above, it is mentioned that Amos is four times older than Sam. So if Sam is 'x' years old, then Amos would be '4x' years old. It is mentioned that the sum of their ages is 86 years. So, Sam's age ('x') plus Amos' age (4x) will give 86 years.

In equation form:

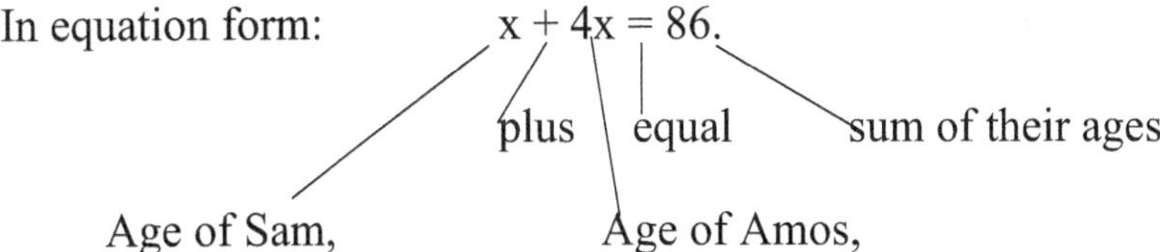

Notice how the equation form of writing in symbols is shorter than the words form of writing. The question in the problem is "how old is Amos?"

We already said Amos is 4x years old. So, if we solve for 'x' in the equation we have formed above, we can then say Amos age is 4 multiplied by the value of 'x'.

Let us solve for 'x' in x + 4x = 86.

x + 4x = 86

(one 'x' plus four 'x' will give five 'x')

So, 5x = 86

Divide the left side of the equation by 5 so as to eliminate 5 from the left side of the equation to leave 'x' alone. Also divide the right side of the equation by 5 so as to keep the two sides stay equal.

$$\frac{5x}{5} = \frac{86}{5}$$

$$\frac{\cancel{5}x}{\cancel{5}} = \frac{86}{5}$$

$$x = \frac{86}{5}$$

x = 17.2

This is Sam's age. So Amos' age, which is 4 times Sam's age will be 4x, which is 4 multiplied 17.2 = 68.8.

So, Amos age is 68.8 years.

You can see from what we have done above that forming equation from a question given in words makes it easier to find an answer. If there is no obvious connection between the facts or things mentioned in the given statement, still look carefully. You might see some hidden connection between the given points which could be used. That is how to go about things to avoid using different alphabets when forming an equation. Check different examples in different mathematics books so as to master different ways of forming equations from statements made in words.

Another example: The sum of the ages of James and John is 27 years. Nine years ago, James was twice as old as John. What is James age this year, and what is the age of John this year.

The problem above shows how a problem given in words could look 'mixed up' and may not be easy to figure out and get the answer off hand. You will see here the usefulness of forming equation to handle a problem that is given in words. Take note of one point: things mentioned in a problem given in words are usually useful for finding a solution. Things are usually not mentioned for no reason. But still always look carefully for what you need.

In the above problem, you can see it is said that the sum of the ages of James and John is 27. Look for a connection between their ages; it is stated that 9 years ago James was twice as old as John. This means that if John was 'y' years old nine years ago, then James would be '2y' years old nine years ago. But that was nine years ago. From that time till date, John's age would have increased by 9 years. So his age this year will be y + 9 years. James age would also have increased by 9 years from that time till date. His age this year would be 2y + 9 years. So, the sum of their ages this year would be y + 9 + 2y + 9. It is stated that the sum of their ages this year is 27. So, y + 9 + 2y + 9 will be equal to 27.

In equation form:

$$y + 9 + 2y + 9 = 27$$

Arranging the items properly;

$$y + 2y + 9 + 9 = 27$$

$$\therefore 3y + 18 = 27$$

We can now solve for 'y' so as to get the age of John 9 years ago, since we used 'y' to stand for his age in 9 years ago. After we get it, we can easily know his age this year.

$$3y + 18 = 27$$

Eliminate 18 from the left side of the equation using the usual method.

$$3y + 18 - 18 = 27 - 18$$

$$3y + 0 = 27 - 18$$

$$3y = 27 - 18 = 9$$

$$3y = 9$$

Divide the left side of the equation by 3 so as to remove the 3 that is multiplying 'y' on that side. Also divide the right side of the equation by 3 so as to keep the two sides stay equal.

$$\frac{3y}{3} = \frac{9}{3}$$

$$\frac{3y}{3} = \frac{9}{3}$$

$$y = \frac{9}{3} = 3$$

$$y = 3.$$

So John was 3 years old 9 years ago. He would be 3 + 9 years old this year (which is 12 years old). James age 9 years ago would be 2y which is 2 x 3 = 6 years old. That was nine years ago. This year he would be 6 + 9 years old = 15 years old.

Example 3:

How much less than 180 is the sum of 99 and 70?

When a problem is given in words, try to understand what the statement means. This way, you will know how to proceed. In this problem they are asking that if you have the sum of 99 and 70 (meaning if you add 99 and 70), by how much would it be smaller than 180. This is to say: what is the difference between 180 and the sum of 99 and 70. From your understanding, you can proceed to form an equation.

Solution: Let the amount by which the sum of 99 and 70 is less than 180 be called 'x'.

Then, $180 - (99 + 70) = x$

(This to say the difference between 180 and the sum of 99 and 70 is taken as 'x' until we find what it is).

$180 - 169 = x$

$11 = x$

$x = 11$

So the sum of 99 and 70 is less than 180 by 11.

Sometimes a problem given in words could be in such a way that you would have to use a part of it to form an equation to solve for something which you can then next use to form another equation to get your final answer. See an example of such below.

Example (4): *the sum of the ages of Tom and Ellis is 60 years. Tom is twice as old as Ellis. If Tom's older sister is 43 years old, by how many years is she older than Tom?*

You can see that the question asked in this problem is: 'how many years is Tom's older sister older than Tom?'

It is mentioned that Tom's older sister is 43 years old. So if we get Tom's age, we can go on to subtract it from his sister's age to know by how many years his sister is older. Let us first work out Tom's age. We can use the statement about the ages of Tom and Ellis to find Tom's age. It is stated that the sum of their ages is 60 years and Tom is twice older than Ellis. This is a connection we would use to get Tom's age.

Let Ellis age be 'x', then Tom's age would be '2x'.

Ellis' age plus Tom's age is 60.

So, x + 2x = 60

(One 'x' plus '2x' gives '3x')

3x = 60

Work to get x from 3x

$$\frac{3x}{3} = \frac{60}{3}$$

$$\frac{\cancel{3}x}{\cancel{3}} = \frac{60}{3}$$

$$x = \frac{60}{3}$$

x = 20

So Ellis age, 'x' is 20 years. So Tom's age which is 2x will be 2-multiply-20 = 40 years.

We now have Tom's age. To know by how many years his sister is older, we have to subtract Tom's age from his sister's age. Tom's sister is 43 years old, and Tom's age is 40 years. The difference is

43 – 40 = 3

His sister is older by 3 years.

You are advised to check different mathematics books to see different types of problems that come in words and how they are resolved. This will give you more knowledge of how problems in words can be approached in different ways.

In sciences such as physics, chemistry, economics etc., problems often come in words. In real life situations daily, things to solve with calculations often come in such a way that we have to form an equation so as to easily solve for something. So, forming an equation for a purpose is a thing you will be doing every now and then. Just keep in mind that when forming an equation, any figure you are not yet sure of is to be represented with an alphabet (an unknown). You would later know the value of the unknown through handling of the equation you formed. It is wise to try using only one unknown when forming an equation. Look for a relationship between the things mentioned in the problem or situation in life so as to use the relationship to re-use one unknown. To give you a clearer picture of trying to use only one unknown when forming an equation, look at the following example.

Jim spent one-quarter of his life in his home town. He spent the next ten years in a university in Germany studying for higher degrees. He later spent half of his life as a lecturer, and spent ten years in retirement before death. How old was he when he died?

This is a good example to show that forming an equation is very useful for finding out something that involves numbers. An equation usually makes things easy when you have to solve for something. In the above question about Jim, you are to form an equation. But it looks like each stage of his life would have to be represented with a different un-known. We have said earlier that using one un-known, if possible, could make things a lot easier. So let us look at a way to use one un-known in this problem on Jim. As earlier said, you have to look for a relationship between the facts mentioned in a problem given in words. In Jim's case here, his total life years is what is referred to in different portions of his life; like "one-quarter of his life", "ten years of his life", and "half of his life". The question of "how old" he was at the end of his life then came up. The common thing in all the portions of his life here is his "total life years", because in each fact you heard "one-quarter **of his life**" and so on (and it is his total life years we are asked to find). So let us call his total life years 'x'. From here you can see that "one-quarter" of his life would mean $\frac{x}{4}$, and "ten years in his life" would mean 10, and "half of his life" would mean $\frac{x}{2}$ and "ten years" again in retirement would be 10. We know that adding all the portions of his life years would give the total life age at the end of his life.

So, $x = \frac{x}{4} + 10 + 10 + \frac{x}{2}$

$x = \frac{x}{4} + 20 + \frac{x}{2}$

Remove everything that has 'x' from the right side of the equation so that only a thing or things with 'x' will be on the left side of the equation since we are solving for 'x'.

$$x - \frac{x}{4} - \frac{x}{2} = \frac{x}{4} - \frac{x}{4} + 20 + \frac{x}{2} - \frac{x}{2}$$

$$x - \frac{x}{4} - \frac{x}{2} = 0 + 20 + 0$$

$$x - \frac{x}{4} - \frac{x}{2} = 20$$

This is the same thing as $\frac{x}{1} - \frac{x}{4} - \frac{x}{2} = 20$

Notice that x is present on each of the items present on the left side of the equation above. With the use of brackets, the x can be brought out of each item and arranged as if multiplying each item. It is a way of manipulating an equation so that every other thing could be removed to leave x alone. You can learn about use of brackets and how to handle brackets in the book "Student's Companion in Mathematics" by Verity,E. So, form brackets so as to have 'x' out of all the things on the left side of the equation:

$$x(\frac{1}{1} - \frac{1}{4} - \frac{1}{2}) = 20$$

But 1 divided by 1 gives 1. So $\frac{1}{1}$ is 1

Therefore we continue our working as $x(1 - \frac{1}{4} - \frac{1}{2}) = 20$

$$x(1 - 0.25 - 0.5) = 20$$

$$x(1 - 0.75) = 20$$

$$x(0.25) = 20$$

Divide the left side of the equation by 0.25 so as to remove 0.25 from the left side. Also divide the right side of the equation by 0.25 so as to keep the two sides remain equal.

$$\frac{x(0.25)}{0.25} = \frac{20}{0.25}$$

$$\frac{x(0.25)}{0.25} = \frac{20}{0.25}$$

$$X = \frac{20}{0.25}$$

$$x = 80.$$

So, Jim was 80 years old when he died. You see clearer here that forming an equation is helpful for solving a problem that come in words. Imagine how it would be like if you attempt to solve the above problem on Jim's age without first forming an equation!

So far in this book, you have learned why alphabets are used in mathematics and how they are used, the use of symbols in mathematics, what an equation is, and how to handle equations in mathematics. You have also learned how to solve for something in an equation.

Chapter 10

Summary

After reading this book from the first page to this point, you now understand why alphabets and symbols are used in mathematics, and the reason they are used wherever you see them in mathematics. You also now know what equations mean in mathematics, and why they are used instead of writing in words in the subject. Remember it was pointed out that equations are used in mathematics for the purpose of making writings shorter and tidy. This is unlike most other subjects where writings are done in words.

After understanding the use of alphabets, symbols, and the use of equations in math, you further learned about the nature of an equation (especially the importance of maintaining the equality of the left and the right sides of an equation), and how things are done step by step in mathematics when handling an equation to solve a problem. This simply means how things are done in mathematics.

Knowledge of what you see in mathematics (this is to say understanding the meaning of what you see in mathematics) and knowing how things are done in mathematics are the basics before going further into usual school mathematics. With such knowledge, things should not be looking strange to you, or be like some tricks to you at usual school mathematics.

There are different branches and different topics in mathematics. All these are usually explained or done with the basic aspects of mathematics you have learned here, and some little more you should learn in a next book to this book: "Student's Companion in Mathematics - Things to know to find mathematics easy" – Verity .E. In that book, you will learn some short cuts used in mathematics, meaning of some words used in mathematics, and some other, but few, important things to know to complete your knowledge of basics needed to find usual school mathematics easy to understand.

After reading "Student's Companion in Mathematics", you should proceed to usual school mathematics textbooks. You should afterwards find what you see in mathematics books understandable, and also be able to understand what mathematics teachers say in a mathematics class. This is because you already know the basics of mathematics, which are the things used in every aspect of the subject.

From here, continue into "Student's Companion in Mathematics – Things to know to find mathematics easy" by Verity. E.

Answers to Exercises

Exercise 1. page 23

Note that any alphabets you use in each answer will still be okay (even if different from the ones in the answers below), provided the equation pattern follows the same pattern in each answer below. In mathematics you can use any alphabet to form an equation for any problem. What matters is the pattern of the equation.

1. $x + 4 = 11$
2. $x - y = x + 10$
3. $3x + x = 36$
4. $x - y = \dfrac{x}{4}$

Exercise 2. Page 72

1. $V = \dfrac{g}{6}$

2. $h = \dfrac{n-6}{8}$

3. $k = d - \dfrac{a}{b}$

4. $g = d\,(u + v)$

5. $t = \dfrac{u+v}{\frac{v}{u}} = \dfrac{u+v}{uv}$

6. $t = \dfrac{w-n}{2a}$

7. $x = (af)^2$

8. $u = d^2 - c$

9. $a = \dfrac{u^2}{2}$

10. $n = \dfrac{25^2 + x}{d}$

11. $c = (at)^3$

12. $a = (du)^n$

13. $u = (ab)^4 - 3$

14. $a = (du)^n$

15. $a = \sqrt{9} = 3$

16. $u\ \sqrt{v^2 - 2as}$

17. $a = \sqrt[n]{c}$